Phantom Tongue

Sundress Publications • Knoxville, TN

Editor: Sara Henning
Editorial Assistant: Macy French

Special thanks to Danielle Hayden and Cass Hayes.

Colophon: This book is set in Baskerville

Cover Image: "Obstructed" by Guadalupe Ramirez

Cover Design: Kristen Ton

Book Design: Erin Elizabeth Smith

Phantom Tongue
Steven Sanchez

ACKNOWLEDGEMENTS

Grateful acknowledgement goes to the following publications in which these poems first appeared, sometimes in earlier versions:

Assaracus: "Standing in Front of the Old Castro Camera Store Window," "Thunder," "Human Breath is Eroding the Sistine Chapel," "Certain Other Infections," and "Etymology of Faggot"
The Blueshift Journal: "In Case of Fire"
Cider Press Review: "After Bobby Jindal Posed as White"
The Cossack Review: "Phantom Tongue"
Crab Creek Review: "An Apology to My Body"
Foothill: A Journal of Poetry: "English Has Approximately 250,000 Words"
Glass: A Journal of Poetry: "The Gunman"
The Good Men Project: "Imagined Letter from My Father to His Father," "You Told Me the Reason I Can't Touch Your Hair," and "Tonight is Our Anniversary"
The Indianola Review: "Paleontology"
Luna Luna Magazine: "The Prelude to Orpheus" and "Lethe"
Nimrod: "Photograph of Our Shadows," "Lent," and "The Anatomy of Your Voice"
Poet Lore: "On the Seventh Day" and "What I Didn't Tell You"
Reed Magazine: "Even If There Is No God"
Rogue Agent: "Calafia" and "Passing"
RiverSedge: "La Llorona" and "Past Tense"
Tahoma Literary Review: "Joshua Tree"
Tinderbox Poetry Journal: "The UpStairs Lounge"
Wilde Magazine: "Elephants" and "Homophobia"
Word Riot: "Approaching El Arco / Reloj Monumental" and "Pretend"

"A Pocho's Pantoum" and "What the Water Gave Me" first appeared in the chapbook *To My Body* (Glass Poetry Press, 2016).

TABLE OF CONTENTS

For Gloria, Ignacio, and Jacob

All night...a truth unfolds.
Anatomy and physiology,
the tiny sensing organs of the tongue—
each nameless cell contributing its needs.
It was fabulous, what the body told.

— Rafael Campo

On the Seventh Day

While my family sleeps,
I lick my index
and thumb and rush
through the pages
of Sunday ads, searching
for glossy men posed
in their underwear—
they look like my G.I. Joe
if his clothes weren't painted on.
These paper men
are caught inside words
they don't even know exist:
*Build Your Own Image
from the Inside Out* or
Who's Getting into Yours?
Studio lights cut
their bodies. Shadows
define each muscle.
Their abdominals taper
to a V and direct me to touch
their arrowheads. I make
incisions with left-handed scissors
below their jawlines
that I attach to thick necks
rising from trapezius muscles
built like pyramids. I climb
these constellations
spread across my bed,
sever their waists
from torsos, remove
their briefs, roll
my glue out of its sheath
and paste the wide shoulders
of Hanes models against

lean torsos wearing Fruit
of the Loom. I fasten
the legs of the Cheetah
models with the white tip
of my magic wand.
I've learned to hide these men inside
the pages of my dictionary,
where words always cling
to their wet curves
like the newspaper ink
on my hands, headlines
and stories staining my skin.

Joshua Tree

Even with its trunk arched back
and boughs splayed out

like fingers extended from an open palm,
I'd never mistake this position for praise

though its name is biblical like my own: *Steven*—
the first man to die in God's name, chosen

by my mother who didn't want my name
to sound Mexican. *Spanish is dirty,*

dirty as the soil that insulates roots,
dirty as my left hand after writing

in pencil. And now, when I speak
to anybody in Spanish, I'm an imposter.

My thick accent breaks the legs
beneath each letter and leaves my words

disfigured like that first martyr
after he was stoned and whipped, his face tilted

toward the sky, warm blood escaping
his mouth, open and silent.

Lent

I gave up masturbation—
I thought it would bring me closer
to an orgasm that would make God
come from my lips like a hushed prayer
under my breath. I'd give him praise
like the Pastor said, as if he actually lived
in the cavity of my chest
pounding away at the walls
of my left and right atriums, my striated
doors pulsing as he shouts *Listen!*
If anyone hears my voice and opens the door,
I shall come unto him and dine
with him, and he with me. I imagined
he looked like Gil, the Pastor's son
who was Jesus in the Easter plays,
hanging annually on the crucifix
revealing his abdominals like two sets
of knuckles pressed together, the way
a person can measure two human hearts.
It looked painful, Gil's body tearing
down the middle like that, his torso
ready to rip open and expose
his lungs like a pair of perched doves
inhaling blood and exhaling
salvation through tightened throats.

Pretend

Halloween, 2015

Dressed like a Spartan foot soldier,
your arms and calves flex
in the gaps of your polyester armor

and a long sword hangs
below your waist. I reach
for it and whisper *Let's be real*

Ancient Greeks tonight
even if I'm not Greek,
but a reaper that follows behind you

far enough to pretend we aren't dating
in front of your colleagues and clients.
But I'm not your unnamed shadow.

Imagine what it would've been like
to lay on our backs and read constellations
as if they were sacred, Homeric epics

spread across the sky, nothing
but night between us. Or maybe,
we'd both wear nothing

but togas that trace our contours,
the parts of us we're told to keep hidden.
Imagine casting off those togas

onto low hanging branches
like discarded sails, excess weight
torn from our bodies, two ships

splintering inside of each other,

taking on water and sand and sinking
to the bottom of the Ionian Sea.

Our bodies aren't vessels. Pretend
we're wooden men mounted
to different prows, carved by other men,

the precision of their blades defining
our bodies; we'd remember
their careful hands that hoisted us

into our proper place as figureheads.
We're sinking. The bows of these ships
are breaking and nobody will come

to salvage us. We have to be willing to fracture
ourselves, to sever our palms
and cleave our backs from this ship

that no longer sails. If you do,
I will find you. If you lose consciousness,
I will hold you around your waist—

my splintered arm around
your ruptured back—and carry you
to the surface. We will reach open air,

root our toes into the soft shoreline
and kiss with the parts of us
that were never broken.

An Apology To My Body

Afraid of growing darker like my mother
warned, I slid her razor down my arm
to remove the sun beaten layer of skin,
each pigment in my flesh trapping sunlight

like chloroplasts in the leaves of grapevines
and strawberries. In the fields, she plucked
fruit like feathers from the back of her rooster,
its head tucked between red and blue

wings, the color of her hands, bruised
and swollen. I wanted to break that bird's
neck, sever its skull from its spine, pull
each vertebra from the flesh and feel

each rib snag on muscle tissue like deep
rooted weeds. I would hold the deflated breast
in my palm and wash its soft skin, pale
as my scars, the color I wanted to be.

Passing

One Of The Guys

Are you white or a wetback?
He asks with a rock

that fills his ten-year-old palm.
I'm just like you. I answer

the way I've been taught to speak,
each word precise as stone.

Grab another rock.
I dig in the damp soil

and clutch a large dirt clod.
Throw it at his head.

He points to Luis digging
tunnels in the playground sand

with a spork he saved from lunch.
I clench the dirt clod,

close my eyes, and throw.
It explodes in my raised hand.

Boy Scout

My lure cracks the lake's glassy surface, enticing
the brown trout with a single artificial fly.

His lipless gold mouth consumes the lie
that hooks into his tender jowls.

I feel the rest of his life in this wire, taut
like string between two plastic cups.

Does he hear my heart tightening its pace,
a fist that will not let go?

Cover Girl

My mother's compact
is turquoise and brilliant

like a scarab shell plucked
from the chest of a mummy

I want to unravel. My skin
is darker than this powder

so I rub the soft brown disk
over my forehead, down my cheeks,

and to the base of my neck,
preparing my body for a ritual

I don't quite understand.
I extract the mascara brush

from its green and pink tube,
apply it to my lashes, close

my eyes, and the viscous
black honey seems to seal

my eyelids shut. I open
my eyes and feel each top lash

unstitch itself from the bottom.
In the mirror, my face is beautiful.

I grab a brown pencil, draw
myself a new pair of lips

and fill them with the brightest red
I can find. My mother's skirts

are too big for my waist,
so I wear her Dorothy heels

to match my mouth. I sway
as I walk onto the linoleum.

Each click from these heels
echoes through the kitchen,

through the hall, through
my father's open bedroom door.

Metamorphosis

My father taught me to swim
      by throwing me into Kings
River where plants have held many children
      before me. Inner tubes floated
above like black clouds. I reached
      for them, my fingers sinking
 into the deep tread I gripped
      and pushed, capsizing people
 above. I took their place
      lying in the tube's open mouth,
a black halo.
      My arms, nostrils,
and throat burned.

Instructions

Hold your breath
in the front yard
first, then exhale
carbon dioxide
slowly as you feel
the panic spread
through your chest
and you will last
two more seconds,
maybe three, before
your body contracts
against your will,
forcing the muscles
in your respiratory
system to inhale
everything.

Homophobia

Limp wrists
    like a loose door hinge
        unable to close, open

for anybody to come
    in. Your laugh is a metallic whine
        for attention. Father needs you

to tighten
    yourself. Place a flat head
        to your forearms and twist

the screws
    deeper into the pilot hole
        between your ulna and radius

like a man. Hanging
    from monkey bars
        you say *I'm afraid*

to let go.
    Father says *Stop*
        being a faggot. Your small shadow-

neck held in place
    by his left sneaker, you fall
        in the sand and I hear

you sniffle.
    You grab sand and squeeze
        your hand, each grain

sieving
    through your fingers
        like water.

Paleontology

My father threw secondhand encyclopedias
at my mother's back and she blanketed me

between her and the mattress. Muffled thuds
subsided into soft kicks from my brother

inside her womb. I closed my eyes,
felt her acrylics dig into my shoulders,

and imagined the photo of fossils
in the book splayed open

on my bed where a Tyrannosaurus Rex
assumed a fetal position, her spine

and tail arched into a semicircle,
skull tucked between claws

and into what was left of her chest. Her ribs
pierced the eye sockets of her offspring.

When that six-mile asteroid plummeted
from the sky, did the mother devour him whole

protecting him the only way she knew how
or did she fall onto him after impact

when the earth's surface became molten
and the atmosphere caught fire?

Now, screeching tires are always the sound
of my father leaving, the gaunt match who struck

our street and caused blue light to flicker
in our windows like the hottest part of a flame.

La Llorona

My father's forgotten
who brought him
to America,

at what point
English wrapped
around Spanish

like the rosary
he held each night,
prayers tightening

around his palm
until each word
lost its meaning.

Somebody found him
when he was a boy
walking in the streets

of Tijuana, his mother
absent. The jagged
remains of his living

room window
cut his hands
when he reached

one more time
toward his own father,
dead for three days.

In my dreams,
my father reaches

toward me

and I want to hold him
and rock him to sleep
with the Pacific tide.

I can never touch him,
always my reflection
in water. A woman

emerges and slides
her finger across
his navel

where kelp grows
like an umbilical chord
inching toward his neck,

each bulb
a swollen knuckle
to pry open.

He suckles her breasts
with blue lips. She says
Cierra tus ojos mijito.

She dips his body
inside the water
and holds him still.

En el nombre del Padre,
del Hijo, y del Espíritu Santo.
His breath rises to the surface.

Imagined Letter to My Father from his Father

Abandoned by your mother, you wander.
I'll follow you, a ghost inside your own

reflection. I'll save the suns that settle
inside my bodies: water, glass,

and every surface that holds warmth.
Lap each river with your clumsy

tongue. You won't forget
you came from México, even when

my face sets inside your memories
like the words of my language

you almost learned, everything
hidden behind your pupils, nights

you'll carry the rest of your life.
Ignacio, the roots of your name

come from *uncertain* and *ignite,*
it means whenever you say it

your voice will illuminate
the night. You won't know

how or when you cross the border,
but just howl your name—

others will find you. And still,
others will spend your life

calling you coyote, predator,

chasing you from chicken coops

with a shotgun. And sometimes,
they will leave you with an exit

wound. And when they do,
remember your tongue

heals you, fights infection,
speeds the clot, the salt

of your ancestors rushing,
becoming scabs on your skin.

Approaching El Arco / Reloj Monumental

San Ysidro, California

They say the arch is visible everywhere
in Tijuana, a sign just south of the border

whose metal shines like a northern star
for lost Americans seeking home. Even here

north of the border, I can see it bend
into a halo, into the pink and purple buildings,

rising like a silver sun over the border
wall—that lean shadow stretching

across this beach where children pass
through cold iron bars—first their hands, then arms

and shoulders, each daring the next
to go one limb farther. The bravest keep

one foot on this side, one on the other,
and the border bisects their bodies—

it almost seems to vanish
from chipped paint that reveals

a blue undercoat, pieces of sky
to hold between their fingers.

¿Quieres un elote? a man asks
from the other side. I say

no gracias. He says something else
I don't quite understand. A border

patrol officer points at me, flexes
his finger, and warns *you can't*

stand on this side of the fence,
this is American property. Why

are you here? Show me identification.
Like a parrot, I repeat his question,

each barbed syllable twisting
from my throat. A gull walks

in circles a few feet away, his left wing
broken, upside down; his white

remex makes a path in wet sand
that three offspring follow. I could

hold the gull, stroke his sleek back,
and make a purple sling from my shirt.

But I wouldn't know what I'm doing,
how to reset or mend his bones.

I would just break another one
I try to convince myself, even though

I know what happens if I do nothing.
I imagine my grandmother's voice

filling my throat, *sana sana colita de rana ...*
but I can't remember the rest of it,

the incantation that could heal anything.
Where were you born? Who do you know

on the other side? I articulate two words:

California. Nobody. I can barely even speak

Spanish. *Turn around and raise your arms.*
The children observe me and my silhouette

hangs from the wall's barred shadows.
He presses his hand against my body,

pats my calves, searches my thighs,
cups my crotch, and pauses. *You can leave.*

Walking across the beach, my feet sink.
I try to step inside the footprints of others

and notice another gull, this one dead,
tire treads marking his body, his neck

snapped into a parabola, Tijuana's arc
crossing his flattened chest.

The Anatomy of Your Voice

Only you can hear the rattle of bones
inside your voice, the skull's tenor

tucked around the alto of your vocal cords
like the drumhead of a tambourine,

the dense beat of a palm striking skin.
At ten years old you hear yourself

on an answering machine and realize
why kids call you fag—your vocal cords

aren't strings on a cello and aren't steel
braided cables suspending a bridge,

they're membranes slit in your throat
like silver zils in a tambourine ringing.

Whenever you speak
                    remember to inhale

as if through the gills
on either side of a shark—

seven and seven, two halves of a sonnet
that can turn an ocean into breath.

Human Breath is Eroding the Sistine Chapel

Where else do words tarnish
paint and plaster like smoke

on wallpaper, remnants of strangers
I feel close to? The dark matter

of their lungs and mouths scours
the textured ceiling. I light up and lie

down on the motel bed, becoming
Michelangelo on my back, cigarette

stroking the air. I see the world
like I used to, making cold angels

on the white expanse of my backyard
where I watched winter enter

and leave my body, transforming
words into something visible,

almost tangible, like Adam's left
hand that will never reach God.

Standing in Front of the Old Castro Camera Store Window

For Jack Lira

Is this where you met your lover,
  where he whispered his name
    and address into your ears?

Inside my reflection, a taxi vanishes,
  the heat of its exhaust rushes
    against my calves. I, too, have driven

away from Fresno after my father
  found a man sleeping next to me.
    Between cities, I steered towards K-rails

that curved like the small of my lover's back.
  When my car ran out of fuel, the gas pedal
    lost resistance, the steering wheel stiffened,

I became aware of everyone around me.
  Is that what it will feel like to die? I don't know
    where they've buried your body, but I've searched

in every Fresno cemetery. I've found Orion
  and I imagine you, in the sky, unfastening
    his bright, pulsing belt. I know you can

never step back down from that wooden,
  creaking chair. But Jack, I think I hear you
    when the floorboards in my bedroom tighten.

Thunder

is friction between two bodies
           that touch and leave

a vacuum, the slim space
       between your back and my chest
           when we curl into each other

before sleep, two commas
       or open ended quotation
           marks that nobody knows

how to finish. Tonight,
       thunder is a stand-in for our words
           that fail to talk about cancer,

diagnosis and prognosis.
       Never confuse these two,
           the difference between naming

and what the named will do
       in the body. Thunder punctuates
           the periodic silence

of wandering thoughts
       that always return to a point
           closer than expected.

Thunder is an echo of a soul
       that I want to believe will bolt
           from the ground toward the sky—

thunder is a warning
       that lightning rods can be made
           of flesh and bone, that our atoms

can polarize,
        that our bodies can be drawn to this earth
               and pulled toward the stratosphere.

You Told Me the Reason I Can't Touch Your Hair

and once, I forgot it.
　　　　Our limbs and appendages

rooted inside each other,
　　　holding and tasting
　　　　　the soft soil of our bodies

until I reached your hair
　　　and my hands became
　　　　　　your father's.

Birds flocked
　　　from your spine—
　　　　　their wings arched

ribs. Red-tipped
　　　feathers fell
　　　　　on the sheets

from the ghost
　　　pecking inside
　　　　　your skull, breaking

the yolk of memory
　　　with an egg tooth
　　　　　on the tip of his beak,

your father's nose
　　　　　at the base
　　　　　　　of your neck,
his talons
　　　gripping your hair
　　　　　like an abandoned nest.

Sometimes, you hold my hands,
        place them upon your head,
                and I know this means *I love you.*

And some nights
        you tremble in your sleep,
                caught between two seasons,

and I glide over your body
        to whisper in your ear
                like a wind rattling

dead leaves from branches.

Tonight is Our Anniversary

The interpreter assembles
a galaxy above his head

and reminds me
what you must look like

when interpreting for
coworkers and consumers.

Nobody from that world
knows about us, yet

you taught me how
to introduce myself, how

in American Sign Language
my name is a series of fists,

my thumb a meteor weaving
between my knuckles

before impact. Stars collapse
in the interpreter's hand

and I imagine he's you
up there, introducing us

for the first time: I'm a single
star above your head, looking

down at the years
that pass inside your fists

rotating around each other,
almost orbiting, except

to sign *year* fists must touch,
signaling closure, unlike

the real universe
where distance expands

every year, between moon
and earth, earth and

sun, our sun and the next
nearest star, light years away.

Once, I tried to hold
your hand in the bar

and you pulled away—
we heard a man slam his fist

against the foosball table.
Years later, walking

through the Home Depot
nursery near closing time,

you pushed me away
when I leaned in for a kiss.

Tonight, I'm thousands of miles
away and I can't help but imagine

your hands are in the sky,
one reaching for mine,

the other thumbing
the half-moon like a quarter

into the jukebox night.

Elephants

I pretend to sleep each night
you whisper it in my ear. Your nose

grazes my face like an elephant's trunk
and I think how terrifying it'd be to wake

under the feet of an animal
whose weight can make my stomach

collapse, an animal whose tusks
can carve cavities from my body.

An elephant's heart beats faster
when lying down anywhere

in the Savannah, Indonesia, or China —
even the backseat of a parked car

in the middle of Fresno. Silence
ties the beats in your chest like rope

to bamboo. A northbound train echoes
the thousand feet of a caravan. I lie

still under ivory starlight.

The Prelude to Orpheus

When I kiss you now, it's a crackle
in the light bulb that draws my attention,
the swamp cooler's hum, the humid air.
I'm not supposed to open my eyes,
so I pretend we are kissing
two summers ago, lying on the bed
of your green pickup, waiting for the moon
to eclipse the sun, for the red iris
to disappear behind its dilated pupil.
And for that moment, we stare
directly at the star that brought us
here. Soon, we will have to turn away.
In less than a minute, our retinas will burn
and our brain cannot register the pain
of one hundred and thirty million cells
drying. It will take hours to notice
the damage that's been done
and it will be too late. You brought
your homemade pinhole camera. *Look*,
you said, pointing to the black apparition
sliding across the pavement
then leaving. This is nobody's fault,
this final departure just as natural
as anything else in the universe.

Photograph Of Our Shadows

Hunched like the lightning

                       struck tree, our shadow is

split across this crevasse of sky, our bodies

                       absent, but our mouths touch

against each other behind the lens, kiss

                       almost like two black holes inhaling

light beyond this universe—

                       our last photo together. Remember

some physicists believe

                       every possible universe exists—

we can return to the cemetery,

                       open a bottle of Barefoot Moscato,

talk about death with a sweetness,

                       taste apricot and peach on our tongues,

and I'll hear you whisper *Steven,*

                       come back with me to the car,

it's getting cold out here.

Lethe

Lake Success, CA

Drowning is a quiet thing,
no flail or scream,

just the sensation of fire,
the voice replaced by the need

to breathe. I take another swig
from this handle of Black

Velvet, petals wash over my tongue
and stems and thorns lodge

inside my throat. I dig
my feet deeper in the sand.

The tide rises just above my calves
and pulls me to my knees.

I've lost the urge to move, though I keep
swaying with the Tule Reeds

in the breeze, their whispers coming
from somewhere below me,

the wind's whine carrying
what's left of your laughter.

What the Water Gave Me

1938, oil on canvas, 91x70.5 cm by Frida Kahlo

The closer I move to this painting,
      the more my shadow floods this scene

where a Conquistador ship sails west
      towards the undertow between

my shadow's black core
      and its frayed periphery.

Each step forward drags them
      from the light, their colored pigments

rushing away from me like sand
      on a shoreline beneath my feet.

I step back to remember
      what else my body's darkness saturates,

a second life tethered to my feet,
      and I notice hers, braced

against the tub's cool porcelain,
      touching their own reflection just below

the surface like a perpetual baptism
      where past and present pull her

to walk in two different directions.
      The farther I move,

the more my shadow spreads,
      stretching across these floors,

these walls, around half the earth
        on any given night when the moon

is the only way of seeing
        myself in Mexico, the country

I spent years drowning,
        only to have my own body emerge.

After Bobby Jindal Posed as White

Standing before this stranger,
I become the silhouette

of a fair-faced man who doesn't exist;
I am a dark spot in the middle of the sun

whose brightness surrounds and haunts
me wherever I go, even inside

my own home where my eyes adjust
to light's absence by summoning black floaters

to hover between me and my body,
to obstruct my vision and consume

my skin. They seem to never leave
but settle in melanin like smoke

trapped inside a glass candle jar,
the wick extinguished. Like me,

did this stranger lather his arms and face
with a bottle's worth of skin lightening

lotion, an attempt to make
eye contact with his own reflection?

In this self-portrait, his straight-
legged shadow undermines

his casually bent knee.
Beyond this frame, I imagine

the rest of it sprawled across marble

steps, pinned against alabaster pillars,

kicked by shuffling feet, unable to rise
from the scorching concrete.

Did he, too, learn to survive
by avoiding eye contact, by staring

at the ground and watching
his feet enveloped by the shade

of kids taller and paler than him?
Like me, did he believe his skin

color came from the dirt,
impossible to scrub away?

There's strange comfort in steam
fogged over a mirror where,

for a few moments, my body
may be exchanged for a foggy

silhouette. Or, I can press
my palm against warm glass, wipe

the mirror clean, and feel heat
rise from my own reflection.

English Has Approximately 250,000 Words

If words were rationed like canned meat
or rice and beans, I'd savor each syllable

like my grandma's chile verde that left
something to taste even when it was gone.

We would borrow words from neighbors
the way she asked ours for tortillas

or milk when we were running low.
We waited for my grandpa to return

with something more than an empty bottle
between his calloused hands. Bruises

sometimes rose on his neck
like swollen tongues. She would scrape

his cold plates into ours. Refried beans
hardened on our spoons like stories

about where Grandpa went—he got lost
in the fields of whatever fruit was in season,

or maybe his blue pickup needed gas,
but he'd be home soon. His other lover

spoke English better than Spanish.
My grandma tried teaching me how to roll

my tongue while she heated tortillas
over the stove's blue flames.

He'd call her into the next room and

and I'd tear a match from the book

and hold it near the fire, listening to the quiet
whir between Spanish and breaking glass.

A Pocho's Pantoum

No hablo Español, I'm sorry. Each syllable
flicked from my forked tongue settles
on the eggshell floor. Airplanes fly
between each question. I swallow

each of her cries. She questions
how my mouth expels Spanish
like rejected prey. *¿Mijito, mijito
dónde está cuarenta y dos?*

I swallow rejection, pray
when I ask *¿Qué pasó, qué pasó?*
¿Mijito, mijito, dónde está cuarenta y dos?
The only other brown person here

is me. I ask *¿Qué pasó, qué pasó?*
and everyone walks past and stares
at the only two brown people here
as if we understand each other.

I want to tear through my skin,
shed it and leave. Her hand
is soft, sheds a memory
of my grandma. *¿Mijito, dónde esta…?*

No entiendo. Lo siento. Lo siento. My Spanish
is my grandma who warned where snakes
lurk in her garden. She taught me
to kill. My Spanish is a language

of apologies that crack in my voice.
every syllable is a question
my voice cracks through the eggshell room.
No hablo Español, lo siento.

Calafia

My mother points at the black vase
glistening under halogen bulbs,
its cracks sealed with gold streams
that almost trickle. *It's beautiful* she says.
I want to take this for her, hold it
between my hands so that its gold
could sieve through my lifelines
as if they were mesh wire
in a miner's pan, filtering gold
from my own body and blood
that I could give to my mother,
gold I could return to her joints.
She smiles, sits, and rubs her knees.
Keep looking. There isn't a cure.
Her immune system excavates
cartilage, creates canals around
her patella, fibula, and femur.
Her antibodies are rabid vigilantes
like California's forty-niners
staking claims inside her marrow.
Rings refract light from her hands
like a pair of silver gauntlets,
her necklaces glint like chainmail,
and I remember who my mother is:
the warrior who grappled with my father,
who taught me to solely use English
like a shield to protect me
from the boys who taunted
the color of my skin. I don't want
to believe in Calafia. If she lived and
shared our bloodline, the Conquistadors
and miners share it too, as if they're the reason
our bodies spend our entire lives
destroying their own cells,

its only method of healing.
With each year, my mother's walk slows
despite the rheumatologist inoculating
her joints with steroids like molten gold,
but she says it feels more like ice,
the sensation of each approaching storm
that makes her joints swell
as if her bones are the clouds surrounding
thunder's crack, the sound of her walking.

Past Tense

My grandma kept a bottle of chocolate
syrup next to her recliner. Each time
I spent the night, she bought a sleeve
of vanilla ice cream cups from the store.

She'd grab one, take her insulin, and wink.
I'd ask her to translate her novelas
whenever someone cried, meaning
every betrayal was in English.

At 10:30, we'd brush our teeth, rinse
our mouths, and she'd sing in Spanish
until I closed my eyes, imagining
small pigeons flying from her tongue,

carrying rolled R's like small parcels
I've never been able to unwrap.
Sometimes, I dream she's still here
sleeping next to me and I whisper

an apology for releasing her canary
when I was little. She never clipped
his wings, thought he might need them.
Now, I'm learning to speak, to tell

the difference between the preterit
and imperfect, escapó and escapaba,
between ella cantó and memory.

Phantom Tongue

A cavity grows inside
        your mouth, a void
                collapsing your tooth:

a broken crown
        exposing dentine
                and a nearly severed neck.

You feel an open nerve
        billow from its canal
                like a Tule reed trembling

between each sharp breath.
        This is why you are here:
                to eat, drink, and breathe

without vigilance;
        this is why you permit this man
                wearing a white mask

and white gloves
        to reach inside your mouth.
                His anesthesia spreads

through your gums, seeps
        into your lips and seizes
                your tongue, breaking

communication
        between you and your body.
                This white man

begins to speak
        of Baltimore, of burning

cars and shattered windows

as he drills inside
        your tooth,
                excavating pulp and nerve

to ensure you never feel
        this pain again. He praises
                the mother for hitting her son

protesting in the street. He packs
        your mouth with cotton
                to keep your tongue

from getting in the way.
        He says *you're lucky*
                your insurance covers composites;

the white crown
        inside your mouth
                is safer than amalgam

because silver would seep
        into your gums and
                blood, would make your mouth black.

Even if There is No God

Even if there is no God, I still love
how light cracks through cathedral
glass, casting faces in red and blue

as if these windows are nothing
more than the pair of 3D glasses
I once ordered from a comic book

thinking they'd have x-ray powers;
I wore them to church so I could see
through the cream colored wall

that separated the congregation
from the urinals, so I could stare at
the men in slacks and polyester pants

until my grandmother squeezed my hand.
Her fingers always feel cold to me now.
I think about my own body, visible

despite the absence between my atoms,
strung together like beads in a rosary.
I'm sitting in this pew, avoiding

the gaze of strangers.
My grandmother asked me to come
so that she could teach me to pray,

so that I might learn the vocabulary
of the dead. I hear rattling
inside her chest and a chill

reaches down my back
as if a hand were slowly holding

and releasing each vertebra in prayer.

She said she felt the spirit come over her
in the hospital last week, after
she fell for the second time, and I couldn't

tell her it might just be the IVs
rehydrating her body, filling her
veins until they swelled in her hands

and wrists, something inside
her trying to escape.

The Gunman

Orlando, June 12, 2016

Imagine:
    the four chambers of my heart
        each loaded with a bullet,
    each beat another revolution
      in my chest,
my throat
    a barrel,
      my curled tongue
          a trigger.
      I believe
        in spirits,
in every *fag*
    and *queer*
      I've heard
        and allowed
          to pass through my body
      and into the next.
I believe
    in possession,
      believe each metal slug
    entering our bodies
        tonight is a history
    we can't escape,
        forged in factories
    across this country
          by men
      who feel threatened
          by love.
And when I stare
      into my reflection
        one last time tonight,
    I know each pupil

will become an exit
                    wound.
                              I've spent my life
              learning to lie
                    to myself,
                              but tonight
the truth
        will enter my body,
                    will hurt,
                              will kill,
                                        will leave
an echo.

In Case of Fire

            Don't panic. Shatter
the glass
            between you
                        and the extinguisher
with your elbow
            or foot;
                        never your hands
or they'll bleed
            like your father's
                        after he punched
a window
            in place of
                        your mother.
Pull the pin
            like a braid
                        of hair.
Squeeze the handle
            like a small boy's
                        wrist. Break
through the fire
            if it spreads
                        too far. Go,
find yourself,
            ten years old, hiding
                        beneath the sheets.
Get him out
            knowing
                        all you can do
is clear a path
            to the nearest exit
                        you might not reach.
On your hands
            and knees,
                        lead him, crawl

with your face
        lowered
                to the ground
below the hem
        of smoke
                as if you're bowed
in reverence
        to this rage—fire
                that never ends,
its embers
        surrounded
                by memories
you've pushed
        like boulders
                surrounding a fire pit,
the barrier
        you need
                between you
and your father,
        you
                and your temper,
ready to lash out
        in the smallest crack
                or lapse
of thought.
        In case of fire
                remember
your father's
        dozen faces
                splintered
in glass, remember
        how sharp
                his eyes can be,
how easy
        your bare foot
                can crush
his face
        into dust,

how even then
you'll carry shards
of him
inside your skin.

Etymology of Faggot

1.

A phoenix perches
on each of my shoulders, wings

drawn from the ink of a needle
that coaxed my body

to heal itself, to rise
and inflame around each new puncture.

Feathers fall down my back
and across my torso, thighs, and legs—

red and blue inked burnings
indiscernible from swelling bruises.

Black dates mark each feather
inside a cloud of smoke

like headings on pages
of a journal I'll never misplace

even after the ink fades
and morphs with a lifetime of use

like a word that's survived
eight hundred years.

2.

Whenever I wander
into the undergrowth

at the edge of Lost Lake,
twigs snap into two

syllables beneath my feet,
and I think about the woodsman

in the middle of winter,
alone in the English forest

gathering, collecting, bundling
anything he could find

to keep warm, how the bundles
became heretics

bound to the stake,
how when a man entered me

for the first time,
it burned,

how when I'm cremated,
I will be one less body, flaming.

Certain Other Infections

Men who have had sex with other men, at any time since 1977 ... are currently deferred as blood donors. This is because MSM are, as a group, at increased risk for HIV, hepatitis B and certain other infections that can be transmitted by transfusion.
—United States Food and Drug
Administration, December 2015

The infections must be Prada heels, hooked
into the side of Hepatitis B's protein coat
like some runway where I design
high-end fashion nobody will wear
outside, like a peacock's tail
flared out on a woman's dress,
making it impossible to sit. Or is it
the way HIV thrusts into human
cells, the way two men can push?
Neither can reproduce on their own.
We have RNA and phospholipid membranes
in common — the way we touch
the world, exchange information
through bilayers of fat and muscle,
unzip our genes, break hydrogen
bonds, and replicate into each other
to feel the rush of what we must keep.

Venus de Milo

The moon casts shadows across her
cool marble chest
where she might have covered herself
if her arms weren't missing.
The eternal stone
dress sags just below her hips
and she recalls the cold chisel
carving her
into the plinth
she pummeled into rubble
with her fists and that heavy
apple he put in her hand.
All night she teaches herself
how to walk,
how to raise her knees
and march in place like a soldier
no man could ever lift. Her
feet begin to crack
the foundation she's been bound to
for centuries. The marble museum
floor trembles
beneath her fallen dress. Windows
rattle inside their enclaves
of bricks that begin to gnash
like grinding teeth
moments before a nightmare is over.
The mason's work is undone
and she steps through the fissured wall,
her pale skin warmer, almost peach
underneath the street lamp.

for Adrienne Rich

The UpStairs Lounge

On June 24, 1973, The UpStairs Lounge, a gay bar in New Orleans, was firebombed, resulting in the death of 32 people who were locked inside. The city dismissed the need for a thorough investigation and disposed of some of the bodies in a mass grave without allowing the bodies to be identified. Nobody was ever convicted.

You compressed your chest and torso
to fit between the bars of the window,

a space no wider than the length
of an average man's foot. On fire,

you fell like another piece of debris
blown out the window. Let me catch you.

Here, jump onto this trampoline
that never came, charge down these lines

like fire escapes, leap into the space
where you'll never have to fall.

But who am I for you to trust?
They say it was another gay man

who started this fire, who doused
the stoop in lighter fluid before dropping

the match. And all that I have done
is write poems, more rooms

for you to enter and never leave.
Let me try something else:

You're in the UpStairs Lounge drinking

an Old Fashioned with Reverend

Larson, talking about Acts and his sermon
on Pentecost. Mitch and Louis dance

by the jukebox blasting Cher and fire
hangs above your heads, calling your names.

What I Didn't Tell You

—for my brother

You can ask me anything,
even about my first kiss,
which was at your age
and tasted like stale beer.
I used to feel guilty swallowing
the pulse of another man,
but now I know there are many
ways to pray. There's a name for
that most intimate prayer:
la petite mort—the little death.
If, when your lover rakes
your back, you recall
the flock of worshippers
surrounding you like raptors
when they learned you're gay,
clawing at your shoulders,
squawking for salvation,
remind yourself you have to die
before you can be resurrected.
Never forget what the Bible says:
when two people worship together,
they create a church
no matter where they are—
which must include
the backseat of a car
or the darkest corner
of Woodward Park.
These are some of the things
I wanted to tell you
that night in April
you called me for help
with your history report

about the gay rights movement.
Neither of us admitted
what he knew about the other.
Instead I started
with the ancient Greeks,
told you it was normal for them,
that for one brief moment
they were allowed to shape
their own history and religion,
organizing the stars, forming
Orion, for example,
flexing in the sky, arms
open in victory, belt
hanging below his waist.
But he was punished
for his confidence,
a scorpion's hooked tail
piercing his body
like a poison moon.
When I see Orion,
I think of you and remember
what it felt like
for my knuckles to sink
into your stomach,
for my fist to collide
with your face. Your voice,
your walk, your gestures
reminded me of myself,
your figure bright and fluid,
creating a reflection
I wanted to break.
And now I see
your body spill open—
Big Dipper hooked
to your ribs, North Star
nestled in the middle.

I reach for that ladle
and drink.

NOTES

"Imagined Letter to My Father from His Father" borrows its title from Joseph O. Legaspi's poem "Imagined Love Poem to My Mother from My Father."

In "The Anatomy of Your Voice," the line "seven and seven, two halves of a sonnet" was adapted from Eduardo C. Corral's poem "To the BeastAngel."

"Standing in Front of the Old Castro Camera Store Window" references Jack Lira, who grew up in Fresno but ended up leaving to San Francisco because his father was abusive and did not accept Lira's sexuality. In San Francisco, he became one of Harvey Milk's lovers. According to the San Francisco Chronicle article "The Making of Van Sant's Harvey Milk Biopic," Harvey Milk spoke crassly to Jack Lira, often calling him "Taco Bell" because he was Latino. Harvey Milk was embarrassed by Jack Lira and decided to end their relationship. After the breakup, Jack Lira committed suicide.

"Even if there is No God" borrows its title and first line from Ellen Bass' poem "Even if there is No God."

"The Gunman" responds to Omar Mateen who murdered 49 people at Pulse, a gay club in Orlando, during their Latin themed night.

"Certain Other Infections" responds to the FDA's original ban on blood donations from men who have had sex with men. Now, the FDA allows gay men to donate blood as long as they haven't had sex with another man within a year of the donation.

THANK YOU

I am grateful to CantoMundo, the Lambda Literary Foundation, and the MFA Program at California State University, Fresno for their generous support that helped make this book possible.

While I will never be able to adequately express my deepest gratitude for the following people, I will try:

Andrea Mortimer Rhoads, you were in the middle of moving, yet you still invited me to sit on your couch and talk about my poems. You were the first person who told me to lean into my sexuality, to embrace it, to face what I was most afraid of in my writing. I don't think you ever knew how important that moment was for me, how many times I return to that conversation, how many of these poems began with me remembering that night. Thank you.

Michelle Brittan-Rosado, Cynthia Guardado, Nancy Hernandez, and Andre Yang, my first poetry family, thank you for encouraging me, pushing me, and challenging me to critically examine my work and myself. Monique Quintana, J.J. Hernandez, Erin Alvarez, Amber Cecile Brodie, Carleigh Takemoto, Sean-Patrick Kineen, Daniel Arias-Gómez, Remy Mason, Stacey Balkun, Juan Luis Guzmán, Ying Thao, David Campos, Brenda Venezia, and Kamilah Okafor, my Fresno writing family, I am incredibly thankful for your friendship, advice, support, and guidance.

Corrine Clegg-Hales, Randa Jarrar, John Beynon, Samina Najmi, and David Groff, thank you for your mentorship and encouragement to pursue these poems. You taught me how to see worth and value in my experiences even when the world insists otherwise.

Anthony Frame, Charlie Bondhus, Jasmine An, Fox Frazier-Foley, José Angel Araguz, and Ruben Quesada, thank you for your overwhelming warmth, support, and advice. You continue teaching me how to advocate and champion the work of writers I love. Thank you for showing me what community means and for including me in yours.

Carmen Giménez Smith, Rigoberto González, and Sasha Pimentel, I cannot thank you enough for spending time with these poems. I am deeply humbled and inspired by you.

Doug Pitkin, Gaynl Potter, Paula May, my junior high and high school English teachers, thank you for teaching me how to love language, for helping me understand at an early age how crucial it is for us to honor, create, and share our stories.

Erin Elizabeth Smith, Sara Henning, and the rest of my Sundress family, thank you for believing in these poems, for taking the time to help me re-envision my work, and for giving these poems such a wonderful home.

Guadalupe Ramirez, thank you for designing the beautiful painting on the cover of this book. Inez Ramirez, thank you for holding me accountable. I'm incredibly grateful for both of your friendships.

Javier Madrigal Jr., thank you for being my go-to reader, for your unfathomable amount of patience (I know I don't make it easy), and for always giving me honest (sometimes blunt) feedback. Most of all, thank you for being my partner. I'm grateful that I've been able to share so much of my journey with you.

To my family, thank you for always believing in me. Mom and Dad, you sacrificed a lot to give Jacob and me the opportunities we had, and I know there's so much more you did (and do) that I don't know about—thank you. I love you.

ABOUT THE AUTHOR

Steven Sanchez is the author of *Phantom Tongue* (Sundress Publications, 2018), selected by Mark Doty as the winner of Marsh Hawk Press' Rochelle Ratner Memorial Award. A recipient of fellowships from CantoMundo and the Lambda Literary Foundation, he is the author two chapbooks, and his poems have appeared in *Poet Lore*, *Nimrod*, *Crab Creek Review*, *Muzzle*, *Glass: A Journal of Poetry*, and other publications.

OTHER SUNDRESS TITLES

The Minor Territories
Danielle Sellers

Citizens of the Mausoleum
Rodney Gomez

Actual Miles
Jim Warner

Either Way, You're Done
Stephanie McCarley Dugger

Hands That Break and Scar
Sarah A. Chavez

Before Isadore
Shannon Elizabeth Hardwick

They Were Bears
Sarah Marcus

Big Thicket Blues
Natalie Giarratano

Babbage's Dream
Neil Aitken

At Whatever Front
Les Kay

Posada: Offerings of Witness and Refuge
Xochitl Julisa Bermejo

No More Milk
Karen Craigo

Suites for the Modern Dancer
Jill Khoury

Theater of Parts
M. Mack

Every Love Story is an Apocalypse Story
Donna Vorreyer

What Will Keep Us Alive
Kristin LaTour

Ha Ha Ha Thump
Amorak Huey

Stationed Near the Gateway
Margaret Bashaar

major characters in minor films
Kristy Bowen

Confluence
Sandra Marchetti

Hallelujah for the Ghosties
Melanie Jordan

A House of Many Windows
Donna Vorreyer

Fortress
Kristina Marie Darling

One Perfect Bird
Letitia Trent